186 JAN VAN EYCK
PORTRAIT OF JAN ARNOLFINI AND JEANNE DE CHENANY HIS WIFE

NATIONAL GALLERY
ILLUSTRATIONS
CONTINENTAL SCHOOLS
(excluding Italian)

WITH NEARLY EIGHT HUNDRED REPRODUCTIONS

LONDON

PRINTED FOR THE TRUSTEES

SIX SHILLINGS NET

MCMXXXVII

HARRISON & SONS, LTD.,
Printers in Ordinary to His Majesty,
44-47, St. Martin's Lane, London, W.C.2

The three volumes of Illustrations to the National Gallery Catalogue, designed by Sir Charles Holmes and issued by the Trustees, have met with a success that justifies their reissue in an expanded form. The present volume, issued in a strong binding, reproduces with about a dozen omissions all the pictures in the Gallery in August, 1936, other than those of the British and Italian Schools.

For easiness of reference, the attributions in this volume of all pictures already in the Gallery by 1929 are taken from the 1929 edition of the National Gallery Catalogue.

The reproductions are in photogravure instead of half-tone as formerly. Occasionally this process may involve a slight sacrifice of accuracy ; but for the student, no small reproduction can ever take the place of real photographs, and for the general public, photogravure makes a more attractive book.

2604 AMBERGER PORTRAIT OF A MAN

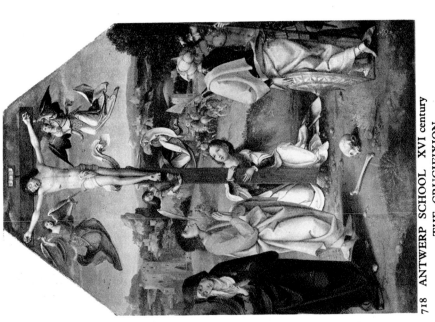

718 ANTWERP SCHOOL XVI century
THE CRUCIFIXION

8

719 ANTWERP SCHOOL XVI century
THE MAGDALEN

1088 ANTWERP SCHOOL XVI century THE CRUCIFIXION

1088A ANTWERP SCHOOL THE ANNUNCIATION

3533 ARENTSZ. FISHERMAN ON THE SHORE OF AN ESTUARY

1346   AVERCAMP   WINTER   SCENE

1479   AVERCAMP   SCENE   ON   THE   ICE

204 BAKHUIZEN DUTCH SHIPPING

223 BAKHUIZEN DUTCH SHIPPING

818 BAKHUIZEN COAST SCENE

819 BAKHUIZEN OFF A ROCKY COAST

1000 BAKHUIZEN SHIPPING IN AN ESTUARY

1050 BAKHUIZEN A SEA PIECE

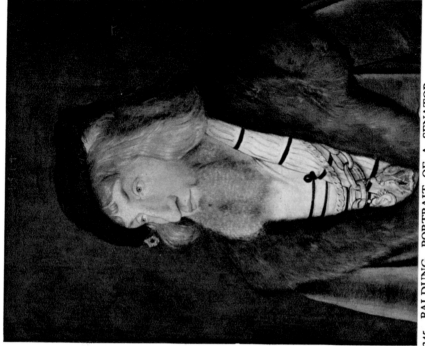

245 BALDUNG PORTRAIT OF A SENATOR

1427 BALDUNG THE DEAD CHRIST: A PIETA

1232 BALDUNG PORTRAIT OF A MAN

3164 BASSEN CHURCH INTERIOR

1311 BEERSTRAATEN THE CASTLE OF MUIDEN: WINTER

1481 BEGA THE PHILOSOPHER

655 BENSON THE MAGDALEN READING

240 BERCHEM CROSSING THE FORD

820 BERCHEM LANDSCAPE WITH RUIN

1004 BERCHEM MOUNTAINOUS LANDSCAPE

1005   BERCHEM   PLOUGHING

1006   BERCHEM   LANDSCAPE

78 BERCHEM, ascribed to LANDSCAPE WITH RUIN

1420 BERCKHEYDE A VIEW IN HAARLEM

1451 BERCKHEYDE INTERIOR OF S. BAVO, HAARLEM

1863 BERCKHEYDE TOWN HALL, HAARLEM

1903 BOEL LANDSCAPE WITH DOGS AND GAME

679 BOL PORTRAIT OF AN ASTRONOMER (?)

3314 BORSSOM GARDEN SCENE WITH WATERFOWL

2551 BOSCH, PIETER VAN DEN WOMAN SCOURING PANS

4744 BOSCH, JEROME
THE CROWNING WITH THORNS

957 BOTH LANDSCAPE WITH CATTLE AND FIGURES

71 BOTH LANDSCAPE :- MORNING

209 BOTH LANDSCAPE WITH THE JUDGEMENT OF PARIS

956   BOTH   ROCKY LANDSCAPE WITH MULETEERS

1917   BOTH   ITALIAN LANDSCAPE

958 BOTH OUTSIDE THE WALLS OF ROME (?)

959 BOTH RIVER SCENE : MULES ON THE ROAD

1090 BOUCHER PAN AND SYRINX

4080 BOUCHER LE BILLET-DOUX

2078 BOUDIN THE HARBOUR OF TROUVILLE

64 BOURDON THE RETURN OF THE ARK FROM CAPTIVITY

1083 BOUTS, ALBRECHT
CHRIST CROWNED WITH THORNS

774 BOUTS, DIRK
THE VIRGIN AND CHILD
WITH SS. PETER AND PAUL

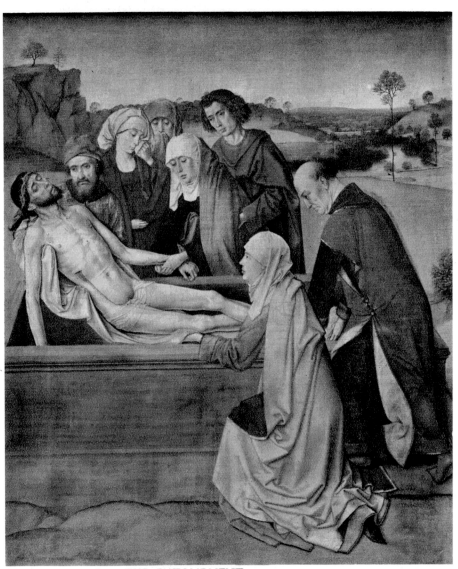

664 BOUTS, DIRK THE ENTOMBMENT

943 BOUTS, DIRK PORTRAIT OF A MAN

2595 BOUTS, DIRK THE VIRGIN AND CHILD

1423 BRAY PORTRAIT OF A LADY

208 BREENBERGH THE FINDING OF MOSES

2549 BREKELENKAM THE TAILOR'S SHOP

1329 BREKELENKAM AN INTERIOR WITH FIGURES

2550 BREKELENKAM
A WOMAN ASLEEP IN A CHAIR

4029 BRIL, ascribed to DIANA AND CALLISTO

2569 BROUWER THREE BOORS DRINKING

3547 BRUEGHEL, JAN THE ELDER THE ADORATION OF THE KINGS

1881 BRUEGHEL, JAN THE ELDER, ascr. to THE GARDEN OF EDEN

659 BRUEGHEL, JAN THE YOUNGER
PAN AND SYRINX

3556 BRUEGHEL, PIETER THE ELDER THE ADORATION OF THE KINGS

3225 BRUSSEL FLOWER PIECE

2605 BRUYN PORTRAIT OF DR. FUCHSIUS

3903 BRUYN
S. JOHN AND THE HOLY WOMEN

2731 BUITEWEG LANDSCAPE

2613 BURGUNDIAN SCHOOL
PORTRAIT OF PHILIP "THE HANDSOME" AND HIS SISTER MARGARET

1292 BYLERT A FAMILY GROUP

2597   CALCAR   THREE VENETIANS AND A CHILD

1241   CAMPAÑA
S. MARY MAGDALENE HEARS THE PREACHING OF CHRIST

1086 CAMPIN (SCHOOL)
CHRIST APPEARING TO MARY

2608 CAMPIN
THE VIRGIN AND CHILD WITH TWO ANGELS

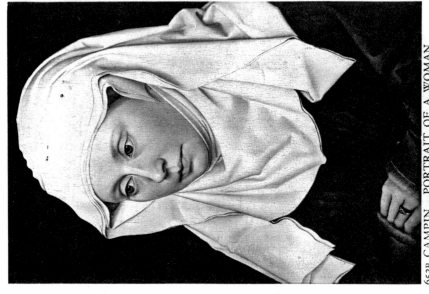

653B CAMPIN   PORTRAIT OF A WOMAN
IN A WHITE HEAD-DRESS

653A CAMPIN
PORTRAIT OF A MAN IN A RED TURBAN

2609 CAMPIN THE VIRGIN AND CHILD WITH A FIRESCREEN

865   CAPPELLE   A COAST SCENE

964   CAPPELLE   A RIVER SCENE WITH SAILING BOATS

965 CAPPELLE A RIVER SCENE WITH A STATE BARGE

966 CAPPELLE A RIVER SCENE

967 · CAPPELLE   SHIPPING

2586   CAPPELLE   A COAST SCENE WITH A BOAT LANDING PASSENGERS

2587 CAPPELLE A CALM

2588 CAPPELLE A DUTCH GALLIOT

4456 CAPPELLE   VESSELS BECALMED

3647 CASTILLO Y SAAVEDRA   THE HOLY FAMILY

798 CHAMPAIGNE, P. DE
THREE PORTRAITS OF CARDINAL RICHELIEU

1449 CHAMPAIGNE, P. DE
PORTRAIT OF CARDINAL RICHELIEU

2291 CHAMPAIGNE, P. DE
PORTRAIT OF CARDINAL DE RETZ

1258 CHARDIN   A STUDY OF STILL LIFE

4077 CHARDIN   THE LESSON

4078 CHARDIN   A HOUSE OF CARDS

1664   CHARDIN   LA FONTAINE

2593   CHRISTUS

PORTRAIT OF A YOUNG MAN

696 CHRISTUS
PORTRAIT OF MARCO BARBARIGO

2602 CHRISTUS, ascribed to
PORTRAIT OF A MAN WITH A RING IN HIS
HAND

2159 CLAEISSINS, ascribed to   THE NATIVITY

2592 CLAESZ.   FRUIT PIECE

2 CLAUDE   LANDSCAPE: CEPHALUS AND PROCRIS

5 CLAUDE   A SEAPORT AT SUNSET

12 CLAUDE LANDSCAPE: MARRIAGE OF ISAAC AND REBECCA

14 CLAUDE SEAPORT: EMBARKATION OF THE QUEEN OF SHEBA

6 CLAUDE
DAVID AT THE CAVE OF ADULLAM: "THE CHIGI CLAUDE"

19 CLAUDE   LANDSCAPE: NARCISSUS AND ECHO

30 CLAUDE SEAPORT: EMBARKATION OF S. URSULA

1018 CLAUDE AENEAS AT DELOS

58 CLAUDE
LANDSCAPE WITH GOATHERD AND GOATS

55 CLAUDE LANDSCAPE: DEATH OF PROCRIS

61 CLAUDE LANDSCAPE WITH FIGURES

1319 CLAUDE, ascribed to LANDSCAPE WITH VIEW OF ROME

660 CLOUET, School of PORTRAIT OF A MAN

1190 CLOUET, School of PORTRAIT OF A BOY

2576 CODDE PORTRAIT OF A MAN WITH HIS WIFE AND SON

2584 CODDE
PORTRAIT OF A LADY HOLDING A MIRROR

1434 COELLO, ascribed to

A BETROTHAL: "THE MORNING COMPLIMENT"

821 COQUES   A FAMILY GROUP

1011 COQUES   PORTRAIT OF A LADY

1114 COQUES   SIGHT

1115 COQUES HEARING

1116 COQUES TOUCH

1117 COQUES SMELL

1118 COQUES TASTE

2527   COQUES   PORTRAIT OF A MAN

2610   CORNEILLE DE LYON
PORTRAIT OF ANTOINE DE BOURBON

2611 CORNEILLE DE LYON
PORTRAIT OF A MAN IN BLACK

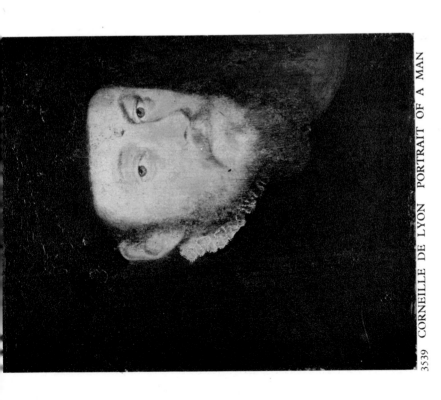

3539 CORNEILLE DE LYON PORTRAIT OF A MAN

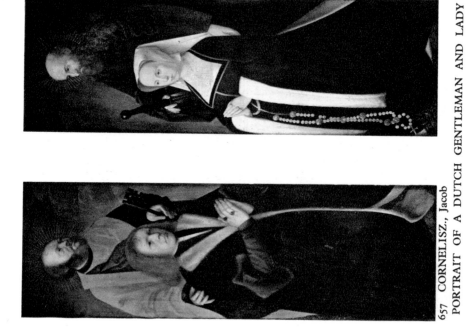

657   CORNELISZ., Jacob
PORTRAIT OF A DUTCH GENTLEMAN AND LADY

2209   CORNELISZ., ascribed to
PORTRAIT OF EDZARD I, 2nd COUNT OF EAST
FRIESLAND

2625 COROT THE BENT TREE

3285 COROT THE CLAUDIAN AQUEDUCT

3816 COROT A HORSEMAN IN A WOOD

4733 COROT PORTRAIT OF A WOMAN

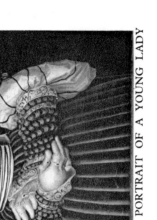

291 CRANACH PORTRAIT OF A YOUNG LADY

1925 CRANACH PORTRAIT OF A MAN

2925 CRANACH CHARITY

3922 CRANACH JEALOUSY

53 CUYP, A.   LANDSCAPE: CATTLE AND FIGURES, EVENING

797 CUYP, A.   PORTRAIT OF A MAN

822 CUYP, A.   HORSEMAN AND COWS IN A MEADOW, EVENING

823 CUYP, A.   RIVER SCENE WITH CATTLE

824 CUYP, A.   UBBERGEN CASTLE AND LAKE

961 CUYP, A.   CATTLE AND FIGURES: "THE LARGE DORT"

962 CUYP, A.   CATTLE AND FIGURES: "THE SMALL DORT"

1289 CUYP, A.   LANDSCAPE WITH CATTLE AND FIGURES

2545 CUYP, A.   RIVER SCENE WITH TWO BOATS

2546 CUYP, A.
LADY AND CHILD IN A LANDSCAPE

2547 CUYP, A.   CATTLE WITH HERDSMAN ON A RIVER BANK

2548 CUYP, A.   BOY HOLDING A GREY HORSE

2622 DAUBIGNY   THE BANKS OF A RIVER

710　DAVID　　PORTRAIT OF AN ECCLESIASTIC

1045　DAVID　　A CANON WITH HIS PATRON SAINTS

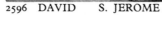

2596 DAVID   S. JEROME

32 DAVID   THE MARRIAGE OF S. CATHERINE

1078 DAVID, ascribed to   THE DEPOSITION

3067 DAVID   CHRIST NAILED TO THE CROSS

1079 DAVID, ascribed to

THE ADORATION OF THE KINGS

1341 DECKER   LANDSCAPE WITH FIGURES

134 DECKER, ascribed to Frans
LANDSCAPE WITH A CHURCH

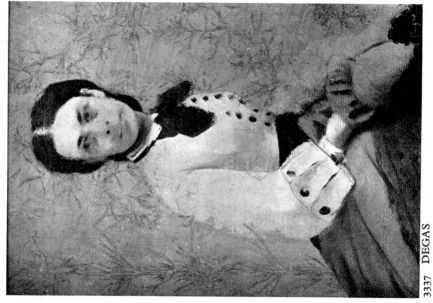

3337 DEGAS
SO-CALLED PORTRAIT OF COUNTESS
METTERNICH

3286 DELACROIX
PORTRAIT OF THE BARON SCHWITER

1010 DELEN   A PALACE IN RENAISSANCE STYLE

2632 DIAZ   THE STORM

3534 DIEPRAEM   A DRINKER MEDITATING

205 DIETRICH ITINERANT MUSICIANS

1305 DONCK
PORTRAIT OF JAN VAN HENSBEECK AND HIS WIFE MARIA KOECK

192 DOU   SELF PORTRAIT

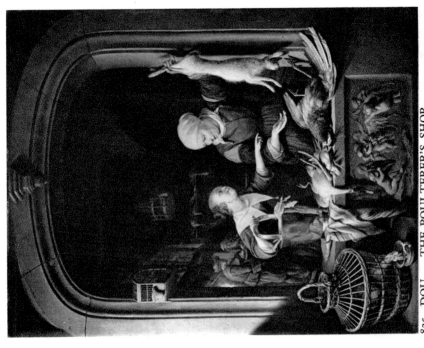

825 DOU   THE POULTERER'S SHOP

968 DOU · PORTRAIT OF A YOUNG WOMAN

1415 DOU · PORTRAIT OF A YOUNG WOMAN

4253 DROUAIS
PORTRAIT OF JOSEPH DE RIGAUD,
COMTE DE VAUDREUIL

1462 DUBBELS   A SEA-PIECE WITH SHIPPING

1810 DUCHATEL, ascribed to
PORTRAIT OF A BOY

2162 DUCREUX   SELF PORTRAIT

1938 DÜRER   PORTRAIT OF THE PAINTER'S FATHER

1652 DUTCH SCHOOL XVI CENTURY
PORTRAIT OF MADAME VAN DER GOES

3459 DUTCH SCHOOL XVI CENTURY
LOT AND HIS DAUGHTERS

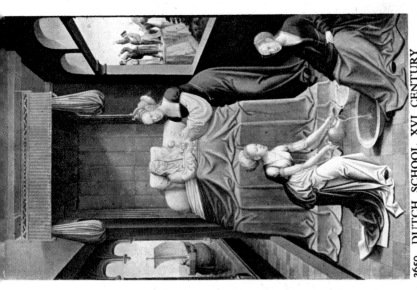

3650 DUTCH SCHOOL XVI CENTURY
THE BIRTH OF THE VIRGIN

3665 DUTCH SCHOOL XVI CENTURY
S. LAWRENCE

140 DUTCH SCHOOL XVII CENTURY
PORTRAIT OF A LADY

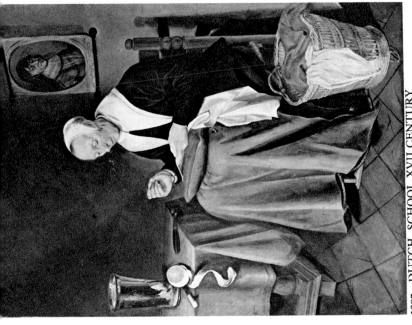

1397 DUTCH SCHOOL XVII CENTURY
AN OLD WOMAN SEWING

1700 DUTCH SCHOOL XVII CENTURY
PORTRAIT OF A MAN

1386 DUYSTER   SOLDIERS QUARRELLING OVER THEIR BOOTY

1387 DUYSTER   PLAYERS AT TRIC-TRAC

49 DYCK   PORTRAIT OF AN ARTIST

50 DYCK   THE EMPEROR THEODOSIUS REFUSED
ADMISSION INTO THE CHURCH BY S. AMBROSE

52 DYCK PORTRAIT OF CORNELIUS VAN DER GEEST

156 DYCK A STUDY OF HORSES

877B DYCK   RINALDO AND ARMIDA

2127 DYCK   PORTRAIT OF MARCHESE GIOVANNI
BATTISTA CATTANEO

2144 DYCK   PORTRAIT OF MARCHESA CATTANEO

3011 DYCK   PORTRAIT OF LADY AND CHILD

172 DYCK   PORTRAIT OF CHARLES I ON HORSEBACK

3605 DYCK   PORTRAIT OF GEORGE AND FRANCIS VILLIERS

1012 DYCK, School of
PORTRAIT OF A MAN

1459 EECKHOUT   THE WINE CONTRACT

1014 ELSHEIMER
THE MARTYRDOM OF S. LAWRENCE

1424 ELSHEIMER   TOBIAS AND THE ANGEL

3535 ELSHEIMER   THE SHIPWRECK OF S. PAUL

3904 ELSHEIMER
THE BAPTISM OF CHRIST

1701 EVERDINGEN   LANDSCAPE WITH A WATERMILL.

222 EYCK   PORTRAIT OF A MAN

290 EYCK
PORTRAIT OF A MAN

1338 FABRITIUS, BARENT
THE ADORATION OF THE SHEPHERDS

1339 FABRITIUS, BARENT   THE NATIVITY OF S. JOHN

3714 FABRITIUS, CAREL   A VIEW IN DELFT

042 FABRITIUS, CAREL
     PORTRAIT OF A MAN IN FUR CAP AND CUIRASS

1686 FANTIN-LATOUR   A STUDY OF FLOWERS

1952 FANTIN-LATOUR
PORTRAIT OF MR. AND MRS. EDWIN EDWARDS

3726 FANTIN-LATOUR ROSES

2104 FIAMMINGO PORTRAIT OF
A MAN IN A WIDE COLLAR

2607 FLEMISH SCHOOL XV AND EARLY XVI
CENTURIES   A MAN HOLDING A MINIATURE

265 FLEMISH SCHOOL XV AND EARLY XVI
CENTURIES   THE VIRGIN AND CHILD

783   FLEMISH SCHOOL XV AND EARLY XVI CENTURIES
THE EXHUMATION OF S. HUBERT, BISHOP OF LIEGE

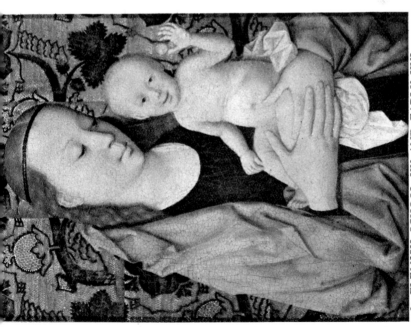

708   FLEMISH SCHOOL XV AND EARLY XVI
CENTURIES   THE VIRGIN AND CHILD

947 FLEMISH SCHOOL XV AND EARLY XVI
CENTURIES   PORTRAIT OF A MAN

945 FLEMISH SCHOOL XV AND EARLY XVI
CENTURIES   THE VIRGIN AND CHILD AND
S. CATHERINE OF SIENA

1036 FLEMISH SCHOOL XV AND EARLY XVI
CENTURIES   PORTRAIT OF A MAN

1063 FLEMISH SCHOOL XV AND EARLY XVI
CENTURIES   PORTRAIT OF A YOUNG MAN

1080 FLEMISH SCHOOL XV AND EARLY XVI
CENTURIES HEAD OF S. JOHN THE BAPTIST
WITH ANGELS

1087 FLEMISH SCHOOL XV
AND EARLY XVI CENTURIES
THE MOCKING OF CHRIST

1089 FLEMISH SCHOOL XV AND EARLY
XVI CENTURIES   THE VIRGIN AND CHILD
WITH S. ELIZABETH

06 FLEMISH SCHOOL XV AND EARLY XVI CENTURIES
THE VIRGIN ENTHRONED

264   FLEMISH SCHOOL XV AND EARLY XVI CENTURIES
A PREMONSTRATENSIAN ABBOT WITH S. AMBROSE

3066   FLEMISH SCHOOL XV AND EARLY XVI CENTURIES
THE VIRGIN AND CHILD

622 FLEMISH SCHOOL XVI CENTURY A GIRL WRITING

3116 FLEMISH SCHOOL XV AND EARLY XVI CENTURIES THE WEEPING MAGDALEN

4033 FLEMISH SCHOOL XVI CENTURY
PORTRAIT OF A LADY IN A PLUMED HAT

3045 FLEMISH SCHOOL XVI CENTURY
THE VIRGIN AND CHILD

4068 FLINCK   PORTRAIT OF REMBRANDT

0 FRAGONARD   THE HAPPY MOTHER

4451   FRENCH SCHOOL XIV CENTURY
       THE WILTON DIPTYCH (OBVERSE).

51 FRENCH SCHOOL XIV CENTURY
THE WILTON DIPTYCH (OBVERSE).

3662   FRANCO-RHENISH SCHOOL XV CENTURY
THE HOLY TRINITY

4451   FRENCH SCHOOL XIV CENTURY   THE WILTON DIPTYCH
(REVERSE).

1939 FRENCH SCHOOL XV CENTURY
THE VIRGIN AND CHILD WITH SAINTS AND DONOR

2612 FRENCH SCHOOL XV CENTURY
PORTRAIT OF LOUIS XI OF FRANCE (?)

2669 FRENCH SCHOOL XV CENTURY
S. CLEMENT AND DONOR

2614 FRENCH SCHOOL XVI CENTURY
A LADY AS S. MARY MAGDALENE

2615 FRENCH SCHOOL XVI CENTURY
PORTRAIT OF MARY TUDOR, QUEEN OF FRANCE

2616 FRENCH SCHOOL XVI CENTURY
PORTRAIT OF A LADY

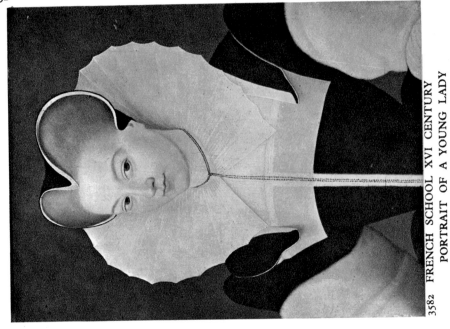

3582 FRENCH SCHOOL XVI CENTURY
PORTRAIT OF A YOUNG LADY

2617 FRENCH SCHOOL XVI CENTURY
PORTRAIT OF THE DUCHESSE D'ANGOULEME (?)

4133   FUSELI, ascribed to
THE BARK OF CHARON

003   FYT   DEAD BIRDS

4081   GEERTGEN TOT SINT JANS
THE NATIVITY

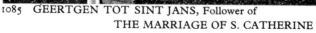

1085   GEERTGEN TOT SINT JANS, Follower of
THE MARRIAGE OF S. CATHERINE

4034 GERARD PORTRAIT OF A FRENCH BOY

195 GERMAN SCHOOL
PORTRAIT OF A MEDICAL PROFESSOR

722 GERMAN SCHOOL PORTRAIT OF A LADY

4573 GERMAN SCHOOL A DEATH BED SCENE

1471 GOYA
THE PICNIC (LA MERIENDA CAMPESTRE)

1472 GOYA THE BEWITCHED
(EL HECHIZADO POR FUERZA)

1951   GOYA   PORTRAIT OF DR. PERAL

1473 GOYA
PORTRAIT OF DONA ISABEL COBOS DE
PORCEL

37 GOYEN   LANDSCAPE WITH FIGURES

151   GOYEN   A RIVER SCENE

1327   GOYEN   A WINTER SCENE

7 GOYEN   A STIFF BREEZE

8 GOYEN   A WINDMILL BY A RIVER

2579 GOYEN   A SCENE ON THE ICE

2580 GOYEN
A RIVER SCENE WITH FISHING BOATS

1122 GRECO   PORTRAIT OF LUIGI CORNARO (?)

1457 GRECO
CHRIST DRIVING THE TRADERS FROM THE TEMPLE

3131   GRECO   PORTRAIT OF A SAINT

3476   GRECO   THE AGONY IN THE GARDEN

1019 GREUZE HEAD OF A GIRL LOOKING UP

206 GREUZE HEAD OF A GIRL

1154 GREUZE   GIRL CARRYING A LAMB

1020 GREUZE   A GIRL WITH AN APPLE

3088 GRYEF   A FALCON

3683 HACCOU   A ROAD IN HOLLAND

829 HACKAERF   A STAG HUNT

1074 HALS, DIRK   CAVALIERS AND LADIES AT TABLE

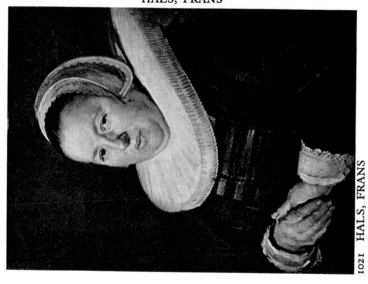

1021   HALS, FRANS
PORTRAIT OF A WOMAN

2285   HALS, FRANS   A FAMILY GROUP

1251 HALS, FRANS   PORTRAIT OF A MAN

2529 HALS, FRANS
PORTRAIT OF A LADY WITH A FAN

2528 HALS, FRANS
PORTRAIT OF A MAN HOLDING A GLOVE

3963   HANNEMAN   PORTRAIT OF A WOMAN

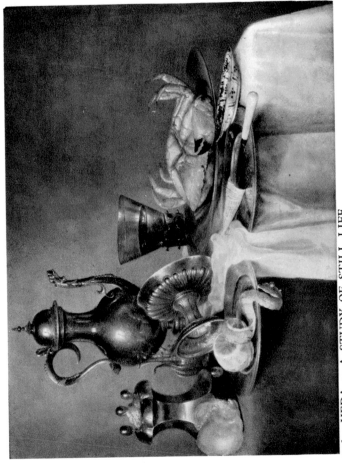

1469   HEDA   A STUDY OF STILL LIFE

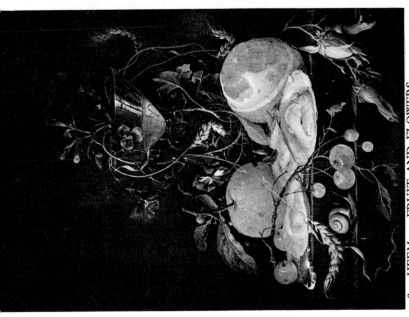

2582 HEEM   FRUIT AND FLOWERS

1243 HEIMBACH   PORTRAIT OF A YOUNG MAN

1248 HELST   PORTRAIT OF A LADY IN BLUE

1937 HELST   PORTRAIT OF A LADY IN BLACK

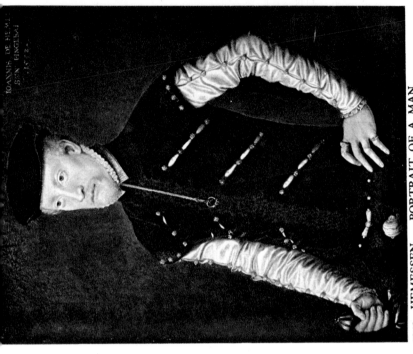

1042 HEMESSEN PORTRAIT OF A MAN

4732 HEMESSEN PORTRAIT OF A LADY

1860 HEMESSEN
PORTRAIT OF A WOMAN WITH A
ROSARY

203 HERP   CONVENTUAL CHARITY

66 HEYDEN   A STREET IN COLOGNE

992 HEYDEN   GOTHIC AND CLASSIC BUILDINGS

994 HEYDEN   A STREET IN A TOWN

993 HEYDEN   LANDSCAPE

4 HEYDEN THE "HOUSE IN A WOOD"

915 HEYDEN A DUTCH CHURCH AND MARKET PLACE

685 HOBBEMA   LANDSCAPE, SHOWERY WEATHER

830 HOBBEMA   THE AVENUE, MIDDELHARNIS, HOLLAND

HOBBEMA   THE RUINS OF BREDERODE CASTLE

2 HOBBEMA   A VILLAGE WITH WATERMILLS

833 HOBBEMA   A FOREST SCENE

995 HOBBEMA   WOODY LANDSCAPE

o HOBBEMA A COTTAGE IN A WOOD

7I HOBBEMA THE PATH THROUGH THE WOOD

1314 HOLBEIN   THE AMBASSADORS

2475   HOLBEIN
PORTRAIT OF CHRISTINA OF DENMARK,
DUCHESS OF MILAN

202 HONDECOETER   DOMESTIC POULTRY

1013 HONDECOETER   GEESE AND DUCKS

3679 HONTHORST
CHRIST BEFORE THE HIGH PRIEST

3315 HONTHORST
PORTRAIT OF A DUTCH OFFICER

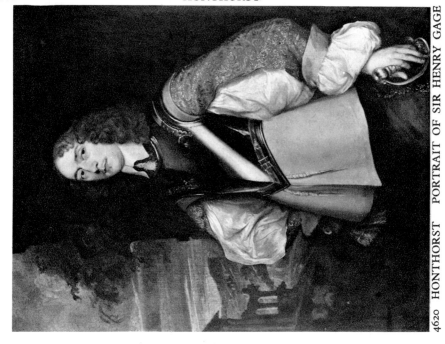

4620 HONTHORST   PORTRAIT OF SIR HENRY GAGE

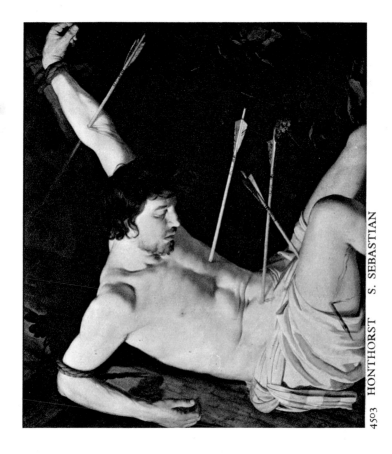

4503 HONTHORST   S. SEBASTIAN

835   HOOCH   COURTYARD OF A DUTCH HOUSE

794   HOOCH   COURTYARD OF A DUTCH HOUSE

834 HOOCH   INTERIOR OF A DUTCH HOUSE

3047 HOOCH "LA COLLATION"

3881 HOOCH INTERIOR OF A STABLE

2552 HOOCH—ascribed to   REFUSING THE GLASS

3832 HOOGSTRAATEN   PEEPSHOW OF A DUTCH INTERIOR

211 HUCHTENBURGH   A BATTLE

954 HUYSMANS, CORNELIS   LANDSCAPE, WOODY COUNTRY

796 HUYSUM   A VASE WITH FLOWERS

1001 HUYSUM   FLOWERS IN A VASE

3165 HUYSUM A VASE WITH FLOWERS

3291 INGRES PORTRAIT OF M. DE NOVINS

3290　INGRES　　ŒDIPUS AND THE SPHINX

3292　INGRES　　ROGER DELIVERING ANGELICA

21 INGRES   PORTRAIT OF MADAME MOITESSIER SEATED

826 JARDIN   FIGURES AND ANIMALS IN A MEADOW

827 JARDIN   FORDING THE STREAM

JARDIN   LANDSCAPE WITH CATTLE

985 JARDIN   SHEEP AND GOATS

1680 JARDIN   PORTRAIT OF A YOUNG MAN

1287 JORDAENS, HANS   INTERIOR OF AN ART GALLERY

164 JORDAENS, JAKOB   THE HOLY FAMILY

1895 JORDAENS, JAKOB
PORTRAIT OF BARON WAHA DE LINTER OF NAMUR

3215 JORDAENS, JAKOB   THE HOLY FAMILY

1280 JUAN DE FLAUDES
CHRIST APPEARING TO MARY

33 KALRAET, ascribed to   THE STUDY OF A HORSE

51 KALRAET, ascribed to   INTERIOR OF A STABLE

3024 KALRAET, ascribed to   WINTER AT DORDRECHT

212 KEYSER
PORTRAIT OF CONSTANTIN HUYGENS WITH HIS
CLERK

74 KONINCK, J. VIEW OF THE SCHELDT

36 KONINCK, P. LANDSCAPE, A VIEW IN HOLLAND

4251　KONINCK, P.　　A LANDSCAPE IN GELDERLAND

1918　LA FARGUE　　THE MARKET PLACE AT THE HAGUE

101 LANCRET   INFANCY

102 LANCRET   YOUTH.

103 LANCRET MANHOOD

104 LANCRET AGE

3883 LARGILLIERRE
PORTRAIT OF PRINCESS RÁKÓCZI

1653 LE BRUN   SELF PORTRAIT

1425   LE NAIN, ANTOINE   PORTRAIT GROUP

3879   LE NAIN, LOUIS   SAYING GRACE

1422 LE SUEUR   THE HOLY FAMILY

3604 LEYDEN   PORTRAIT OF A MAN

1095 LIEVENS
PORTRAIT OF ANNA MARIA SCHURMANN

2864 LIEVENS PORTRAIT OF A MAN

837 LINGELBACH   THE HAY HARVEST

4460 LIOTARD   PORTRAIT OF A
GENTLEMAN IN TURKISH DRESS

705 LOCHNER THREE SAINTS

705 LOCHNER THREE SAINTS (REVERSE)

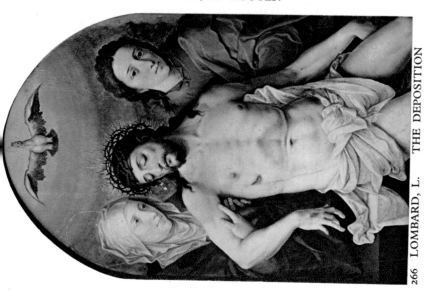

266 LOMBARD, L. THE DEPOSITION

901 LOOTEN RIVER LANDSCAPE

184   LUCIDEL   PORTRAIT OF A YOUNG LADY

289   LUNDENS   " THE NIGHT WATCH "

3571 LYS   MERCURY AND ARGUS

4597 LYS   JUDITH AND HOLO FERNES

656   MABUSE

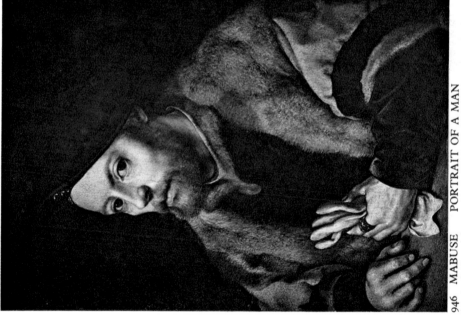

946   MABUSE   PORTRAIT OF A MAN

2163   MABUSE
       A LADY AS S. MARY MAGDALENE

2211   MABUSE
       PORTRAIT OF JACQUELINE DE BOURGOGNE

2790 MABUSE   THE ADORATION OF THE KINGS

9 MABUSE, ascribed to   PORTRAIT OF A MAN AND HIS WIFE

0 MAES, SCHOOL OF   SPORTSMEN REPOSING

1247   MAES   CARD-PLAYERS

207   MAES   THE IDLE SERVANT

1277 MAES PORTRAIT OF A MAN

2581 MAES PORTRAIT OF A MAN

3294B MANET
SOLDIER EXAMINING THE LOCK OF HIS
RIFLE

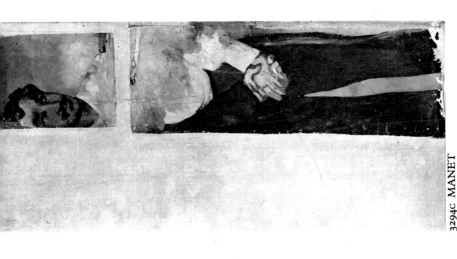

3294C MANET
A COMPANION OF MAXIMILIAN

944 MARINUS TWO BANKERS OR USURERS

1302 MARMION S. BERTIN BORNE TO HEAVEN

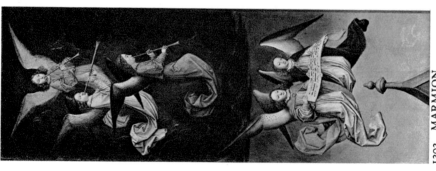

1303 MARMION A CHOIR OF ANGELS

1444 MARTINEZ
PEASANTS WARMING THEMSELVES

295 MASSYS   CHRIST ; THE VIRGIN

715 MASSYS   THE CRUCIFIXION

1081 MASSYS
PORTRAIT OF A MAN KNEELING

3664   MASSYS
THE VIRGIN AND CHILD WITH SS. CATHERINE AND BARBARA

3901   MASSYS
A HOLY WOMAN

3902   MASSYS
ST. LUKE PAINTING

1049 MASTER OF THE AACHEN ALTARPIECE. THE CRUCIFIXION

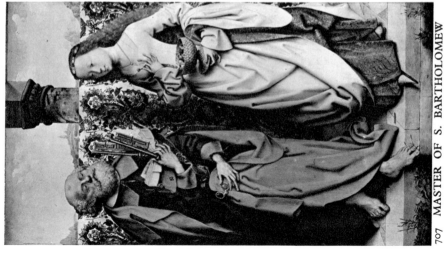

707 MASTER OF S. BARTHOLOMEW
SS. PETER AND DOROTHY

2155 MASTER OF THE DEATH OF THE VIRGIN
THE ADORATION OF THE KINGS

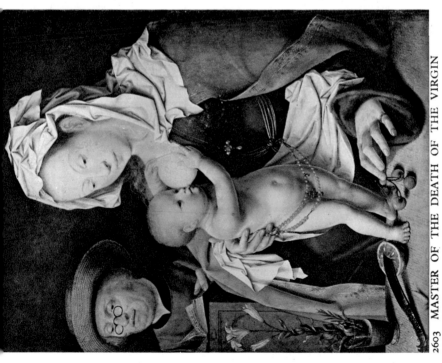

2603 MASTER OF THE DEATH OF THE VIRGIN
THE HOLY FAMILY

2922   MASTER FROM DELFT
THE CRUCIFIXION, ROAD TO CALVARY AND DEPOSITION

720   MASTER OF THE HALF-LENGTHS
REPOSE IN EGYPT

721 MASTER OF THE HALF-LENGTHS
PORTRAIT OF A LADY

254 MASTER OF LIESBORN
SS. AMBROSE, EXUPERIUS AND JEROME

255   MASTER OF LIESBORN
SS. GREGORY, HILARY AND
AUGUSTINE

258   MASTER OF LIESBORN   THE ADORATION OF THE KINGS

256 MASTER OF LIESBORN
THE ANNUNCIATION

260 MASTER OF LIESBORN
SS. JOHN, SCHOLASTICA AND BENEDICT

MASTER OF LIESBORN

257 MASTER OF LIESBORN
THE PRESENTATION IN THE TEMPLE

261 MASTER OF LIESBORN
SS. COSMAS, DAMIAN AND THE VIRGIN (?)

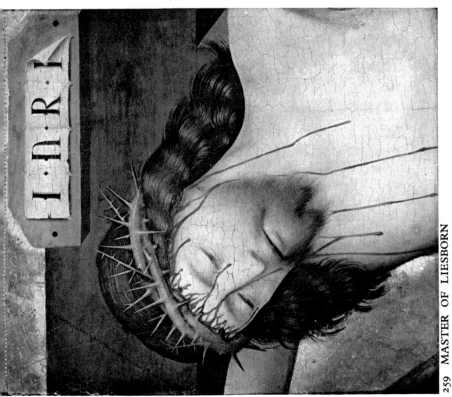

259 MASTER OF LIESBORN
THE HEAD OF CHRIST ON THE CROSS

2152 MASTER OF LIESBORN   SCH: OF.
S. DOROTHY

262 SCHOOL OF THE MASTER OF LIESBORN   THE CRUCIFIXION

2153 SCHOOL OF THE MASTER OF LIESBORN
S. MARGARET

706   MASTER OF THE LIFE OF THE VIRGIN
        THE PRESENTATION IN THE TEMPLE

4092   MASTER OF   MOULINS
        THE MEETING OF JOACHIM AND ANNE

1419 MASTER OF S. GILES
THE LEGEND OF S. GILES (REVERSE)

4681 MASTER OF S. GILES   MASS OF S. GILES

31 MASTER OF S. GILES   MASS OF S. GILES

1419 MASTER OF S. GILES

3379 MASTER OF S. URSULA

250 MASTER OF WERDEN
SS. JEROME, BERNARD, GILES AND ROMUALD (?)

252 MASTER OF WERDEN
THE CONVERSION OF S. HUBERT

253 MASTER OF WERDEN

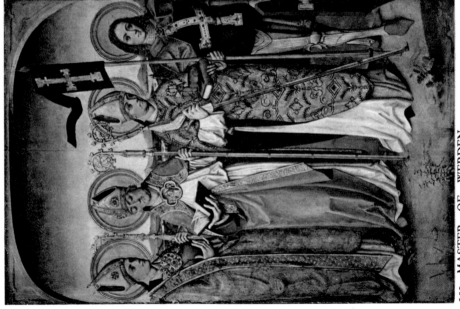

251 MASTER OF WERDEN

376 MAZO A DUEL IN THE PARDO

2926 MAZO
PORTRAIT OF MARIANA OF AUSTRIA

709   MEMLING   THE VIRGIN AND CHILD

686 MEMLING

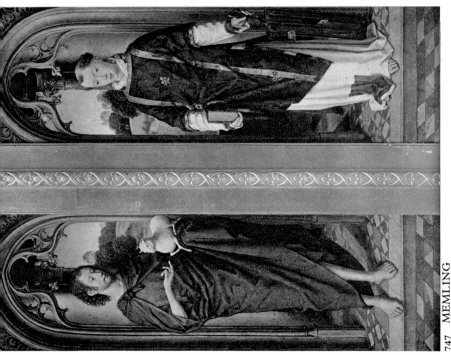

747 MEMLING SS. JOHN THE BAPTIST AND LAWRENCE

2594 MEMLING PORTRAIT OF THE DUKE OF CLEVES

228 METSU THE DUET

228 METSU THE MUSIC LESSON

970 METSU THE DROWSY LANDLADY

2590 METSU AN OLD WOMAN AT A WINDOW

2591 METSU THE FORGE

1447 MEULEN A HUNTING PARTY

2292 MIEREVELD   PORTRAIT OF A LADY

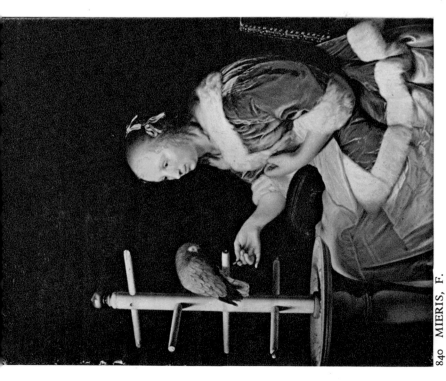

840 MIERIS, F.
PORTRAIT OF A LADY IN A CRIMSON JACKET

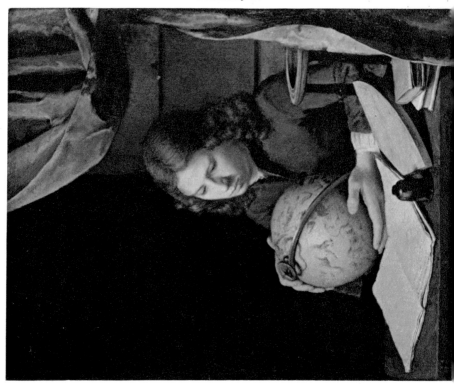

1874 MIERIS, ascribed to F.   SELF PORTRAIT

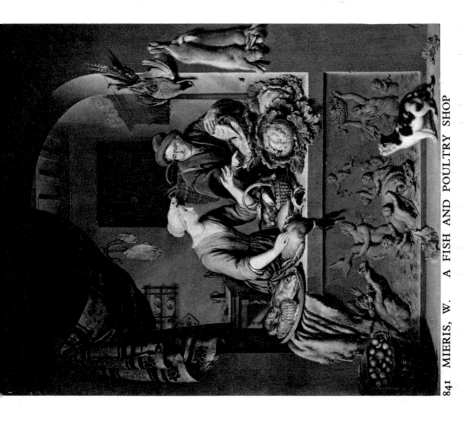

841 MIERIS, W.   A FISH AND POULTRY SHOP

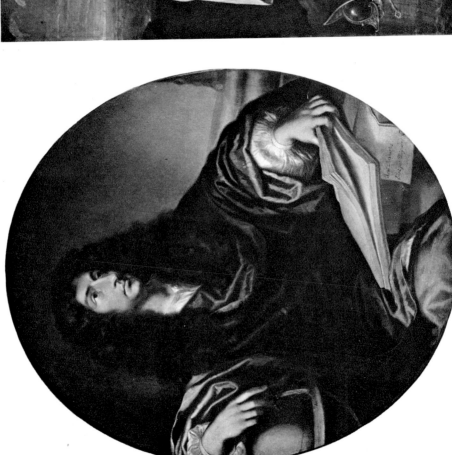

2967   MIGNARD   PORTRAIT OF THE MARQUISE DE SEIGNELAY

2929   MIGNARD   PORTRAIT OF RENE DESCARTES

1222 MIGNON STUDY OF FOLIAGE, BIRDS, INSECTS, ETC.

2636 MILLET THE WHISPER

1293　MOLENAER　　　MUSICAL PASTIME

1231　MOR　　　PORTRAIT OF A MAN

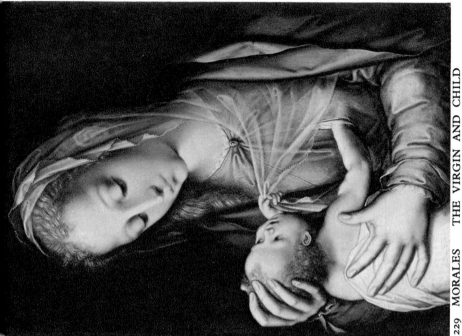

1229   MORALES   THE VIRGIN AND CHILD

3900   MOSTAERT   ECCE HOMO

842 MOUCHERON   A GARDEN SCENE

1352 MOUCHERON
LANDSCAPE WITH RUINS AND FIGURES

13 MURILLO   THE HOLY FAMILY

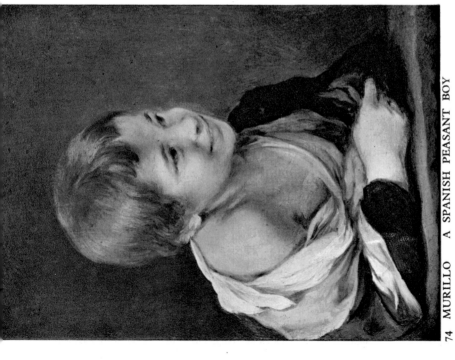

74 MURILLO   A SPANISH PEASANT BOY

3910 MURILLO
THE IMMACULATE CONCEPTION

3938 MURILLO   S. JOHN THE BAPTIST

924 NEEFFS   INTERIOR OF A CHURCH

2205 NEEFFS   INTERIOR OF A CHURCH

6 NEEFFS VESPERS

2207 NEEFFS AFTER VESPERS

152 NEER, A. VAN DER   LANDSCAPE WITH FIGURES AND CATTLE

239 NEER, A. VAN DER   RIVER SCENE BY MOONLIGHT

32 NEER, A. VAN DER   CANAL SCENE WITH FIGURES

9 NEER, A. VAN DER   A FROZEN RIVER

1288 NEER, A. VAN DER FROST SCENE

2536 NEER, A. VAN DER MOONLIGHT

2283 NEER, A. VAN DER   DAWN

34 NEER, A. VAN DER   RIVER SCENE WITH HORSEMAN

2537 NEER, A. VAN DER
LANDSCAPE WITH A HORSE AND CART

2535 NEER, E. H. VAN DER   JUDITH

843 NETSCHER BLOWING BUBBLES

844 NETSCHER MATERNAL INSTRUCTION

845 NETSCHER

1332 NETSCHER

2953 NETSCHER
A LADY AND LITTLE GIRL WITH ORANGES

2954 NETSCHER
PORTRAIT OF A MAN IN A BLACK WIG

4790 NETSCHER   PORTRAIT OF A LADY

2143 OCHTERVELT   A LADY STANDING AT A SPINET

2553 OCHTERVELT A LADY AT HER TOILET

3864 OCHTERVELT THE MUSIC PARTY

3548 OLIS   A MUSICAL PARTY

1137 OOST   PORTRAIT OF A BOY

3649 OOST   PORTRAIT OF TWO BOYS

714 ORLEY, SCHOOL OF BERNARD VAN
THE VIRGIN AND CHILD

3226   OS, G. J. J. VAN
FRUIT, FLOWERS AND GAME

6 OSTADE, A.   THE ALCHYMIST

2541 OSTADE, A. THE COBBLER

2540 OSTADE, A. A ROOM WITH MANY FIGURES

2543 OSTADE, A. PORTRAIT OF A MAN WITH A JUG

2542 OSTADE, A. COURTSHIP

848 OSTADE, I.   FROST SCENE

847 OSTADE, I.   A VILLAGE SCENE

3 OSTADE, I. A FROZEN RIVER

1347 OSTADE, I. FARMYARD SCENE

2544 OSTADE, I.   THE CART

1221 PAPE   COTTAGE INTERIOR WITH FIGURES

26   PATENIR, STYLE OF   S. JEROME IN A LANDSCAPE

6   PATENIR, SCHOOL OF
     S. CHRISTOPHER CARRYING THE INFANT CHRIST

717 PATENIR, SCHOOL OF

1298 PATENIR, SCHOOL OF   LANDSCAPE, RIVER SCENE

1082 PATENIR, SCHOOL OF
THE VISIT OF THE VIRGIN TO S. ELIZABETH

115 PATENIR, SCHOOL OF   REST ON THE FLIGHT INTO EGYPT

3588 PERRONNEAU   A GIRL WITH A CAT

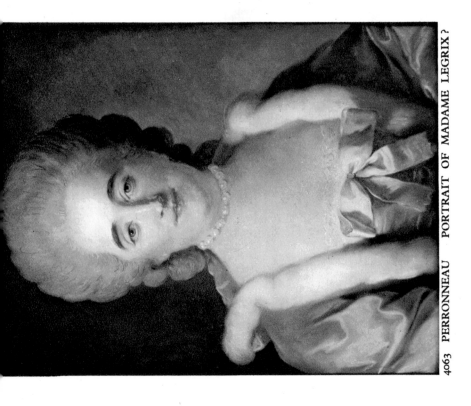

4063 PERRONNEAU   PORTRAIT OF MADAME LEGRIX ?

1061 POEL   DELFT AFTER THE EXPLOSION

955 POELENBURGH   A RUIN; WOMEN BATHING

1294 POORTER   AN ALLEGORICAL SUBJECT

278 POT   A CONVIVIAL PARTY

849 POTTER, PAUL   LANDSCAPE WITH CATTLE

2583 POTTER, PAUL

1008 POTTER, PIETER   A STAG HUNT

1094 POURBUS, FRANS I
PORTRAIT OF A MAN

2295   POURBUS, FRANS II
A MILITARY COMMANDER

31   POUSSIN, G.   LANDSCAPE WITH ABRAHAM AND ISAAC

POUSSIN, G.   A LAND STORM

POUSSIN, G.   LANDSCAPE NEAR ALBANO : EVENING

95 POUSSIN, G.   LANDSCAPE : DIDO and AENEAS

98 POUSSIN, G.   ARICCIA

1159 POUSSIN, G.   THE CALLING OF ABRAHAM

1 POUSSIN, G.   ITALIAN LANDSCAPE

39   POUSSIN, N.   THE NURSING OF BACCHUS

40   POUSSIN, N.   LANDSCAPE WITH FIGURES

42 POUSSIN, N.   BACCHANALIAN FESTIVAL.

POUSSIN, N.   CEPHALUS AND AURORA

91 POUSSIN, N.
VENUS SURPRISED BY SATYRS

5 POUSSIN, N.   THE PLAGUE AT ASHDOD

1862   POUSSIN, N.   THE ADORATION OF THE SHEPHERDS

83   POUSSIN, N. SCHOOL OF   PHINEUS AND HIS FOLLOWERS TURNE
                        TO STONE

2619 POUSSIN, N. SCHOOL OF LANDSCAPE

713 PREVOST THE VIRGIN AND CHILD IN A GARDEN

3422　PUVIS DE CHAVANNES　　　SUMMER

2856　QUAST　　　CAVALIER AND LADY IN A COURTYARD

1848 RAGUINEAU   PORTRAIT OF A YOUNG MAN

43   REMBRANDT   THE DEPOSITION

45   REMBRANDT   THE WOMAN TAKEN IN ADULTERY

REMBRANDT   THE ADORATION OF THE SHEPHERDS

51 REMBRANDT   A JEW MERCHANT

REMBRANDT   A WOMAN (HENDRICKJE STOFFELS?) BATHING

166   REMBRANDT   A CAPUCHIN FRIAR

190   REMBRANDT   A JEWISH RABBI

REMBRANDT   PORTRAIT OF HIMSELF

237 REMBRANDT   PORTRAIT OF A WOMAN

243 REMBRANDT   PORTRAIT OF AN OLD MAN

775   REMBRANDT   FRANCOISE VAN WASSERHOVEN (?)

850   REMBRANDT   PORTRAIT OF PHILIPS LUCASZ

REMBRANDT   PORTRAIT OF JACOB JACOBSZ TRIP

1675 REMBRANDT   PORTRAIT OF MARGARETHA TRIP

2538 REMBRANDT DIANA BATHING

3214 REMBRANDT THE PHILOSOPHER

REMBRANDT, SCHOOL OF
LANDSCAPE WITH TOBIAS AND THE ANGEL

757 REMBRANDT, SCHOOL OF   CHRIST
BLESSING CHILDREN

3268 RENOIR   LES PARAPLUIES

2930 RIBALTA
CHRIST BEARING HIS CROSS

244 RIBERA SHEPHERD WITH A LAMB

903   RIGAUD   CARDINAL FLEURY

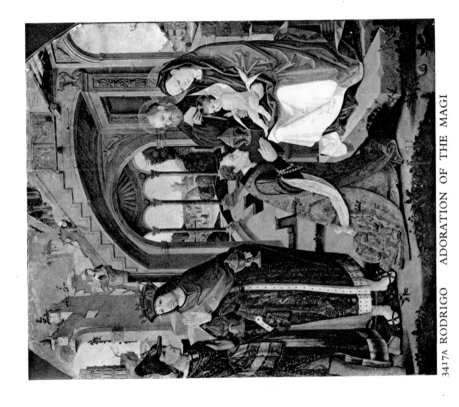

3417A RODRIGO   ADORATION OF THE MAGI

1340 ROGHMAN   LANDSCAPE

2635 ROUSSEAU   SUNSET AT AUVERGNE

46 RUBENS PEACE AND WAR

66 RUBENS   AUTUMN: THE CHÂTEAU DE STEEN

57 RUBENS   THE CONVERSION OF S. BAVON

157 RUBENS   LANDSCAPE : SUNSET

194 RUBENS THE JUDGMENT OF PARIS

278 RUBENS   THE TRIUMPH OF JULIUS CAESAR

279 RUBENS   THE HORRORS OF WAR

187 RUBENS   APOTHEOSIS OF WILLIAM THE SILENT (?)

ɔ RUBENS   THE MIRACULOUS DRAUGHT OF FISHES

852 RUBENS
PORTRAIT OF SUSANNA FOURMENT: KNOWN AS " CHAPEAU DE PAILLE "

853   RUBENS   THE TRIUMPH OF SILENUS

853P RUBENS   SKETCH OF A LION HUNT

1195 RUBENS   THE BIRTH OF VENUS

2598 RUBENS   DIANA AND ENDYMION

2968 RUBENS
      PORTRAIT OF THOMAS, EARL OF ARUNDEL

3819 RUBENS, STUDIO OF
PORTRAIT OF THE ARCHDUCHESS
ISABELLA EUGENIA

3818 RUBENS
PORTRAIT OF THE ARCHDUKE ALBERT

67 RUBENS, SCHOOL OF   THE HOLY FAMILY WITH SAINTS

2924 RUBENS   LANDSCAPE WITH A SHEPHERD

8 RUBENS, SCHOOL OF   LANDSCAPE SKETCH

1865   RUBENS, SCHOOL OF   THE CRUCIFIXION

44 RUISDAEL, J. VAN   BLEACHING GROUND

627 RUISDAEL, J. VAN
LANDSCAPE WITH WATERFALL

628 RUISDAEL, J. VAN
LANDSCAPE WITH A WATERFALL

737 RUISDAEL, J. VAN   LANDSCAPE WITH WATERFALL

746   RUISDAEL, J. VAN   LANDSCAPE WITH RUINS

854   RUISDAEL, J. VAN   FOREST SCENE

5 RUISDAEL, J. VAN   A WATERFALL

86 RUISDAEL, J. VAN   WATERMILLS

987   RUISDAEL, J. VAN
ROCKY LANDSCAPE WITH TORRENT

988   RUISDAEL, J. VAN   AN OLD OAK

RUISDAEL, J. VAN   WATERMILLS

RUISDAEL, J. VAN   LANDSCAPE

991 RUISDAEL, J. VAN   THE BROKEN TREE

1390 RUISDAEL, J. VAN   THE SHORE AT SCHEVENINGEN

51 RUISDAEL, J. VAN   VIEW NEAR HAARLEM

52 RUISDAEL, J. VAN   COUNTRY SCENE WITH A RUINED CASTLE

2563 RUISDAEL, J. VAN   ENTRANCE TO THE FOREST

2564 RUISDAEL, J. VAN   COTTAGE ON A ROCKY HILL

565 RUISDAEL, J. VAN COTTAGE AND HAYRICK BY A RIVER

2566 RUISDAEL, J. VAN SKIRTS OF A FOREST

2567 RUISDAEL, J. VAN   VIEW ON THE HOLLAND'S DEEP

1445 RUYSCH   STUDY OF FLOWERS

1446 RUYSCH   A STUDY OF FLOWERS

9 RUYSDAEL, S. VAN   FISHING IN THE RIVER

1344 RUYSDAEL, S. VAN   LANDSCAPE

1353 RYCKAERT   LANDSCAPE WITH SATYRS

1896 SAENREDAM
INTERIOR OF THE DOMKERK, UTRECHT

2531 SAENREDAM   INTERIOR OF S. BAVO, HAARLEM

2062   SAFTLEVEN   CHRIST TEACHING OUT OF S. PETER'S SHIP

2129   SAINT-AUBIN   UNE PARADE

3154 SANTVOORT, DIRCK VAN   A GIRL WITH A FINCH

3404 SANTVOORT, JAN VAN   JUDITH AND HOLOFERNES

920 SAVERY   ORPHEUS

199 SCHALCKEN
LESBIA WEIGHING JEWELS AGAINST HER
SPARROW

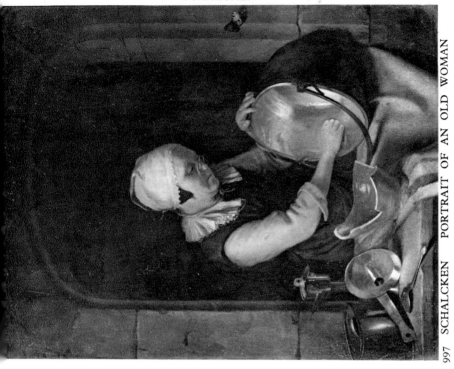

997 SCHALCKEN   PORTRAIT OF AN OLD WOMAN

998 SCHALCKEN   A DUET

999 SCHALCKEN   A CANDLE-LIGHT SCENE

723 SCHOENGAUER, SCHOOL OF
THE VIRGIN AND CHILD

8 SCHWEICKHARDT   CATTLE

383 SEGHERS   MOUNTAIN LANDSCAPE

4206   SEISENEGGER   A LITTLE GIRL

2130   SIBERECHTS   THE WATER LANE

1252 SNYDERS FRUIT-PIECE

1401 SNYERS STILL LIFE

1055 SORGH   PEASANTS AT CARDS

1056 SORGH   A COUPLE DRINKING

4190 SPANISH SCHOOL
THE DEATH OF THE VIRGIN

SPANISH SCHOOL   A DEAD WARRIOR: "ORLANDO MUERTO"

1308 SPANISH SCHOOL   PORTRAIT OF A MAN

3590 SPANISH SCHOOL   S. PAUL

856 STEEN THE MUSIC MASTER

421 STEEN TERRACE SCENE WITH FIGURES

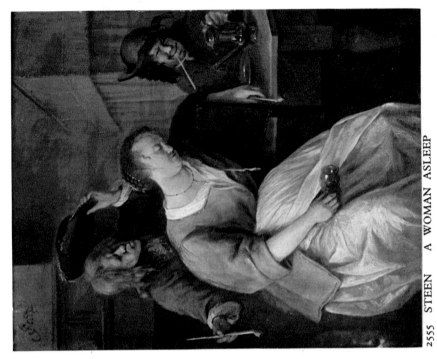

2555 STEEN   A WOMAN ASLEEP

2556 STEEN   THE PEDLAR

2557 STEEN   MERRY MAKERS

2558 STEEN   GRACE BEFORE MEAT

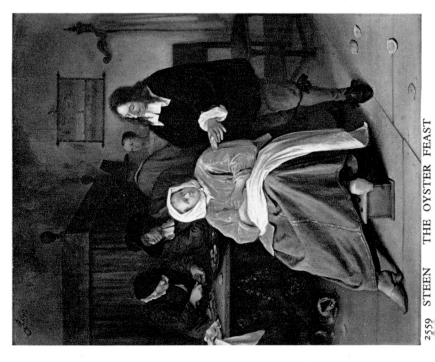

2559 STEEN THE OYSTER FEAST

2560 STEEN SKITTLE PLAYERS

1378 STEEN—After   INTERIOR WITH FIGURES

141 STEENWYCK, HENDRICK   THE PALACE OF DIDO

1132 STEENWYCK, HENDRICK   AN INTERIOR

1443 STEENWYCK, HENDRICK   INTERIOR OF A CHURCH

4 STEENWYCK, HENDRICK INTERIOR OF A CHURCH

40 STEENWYCK, HENDRICK INTERIOR OF A CHURCH

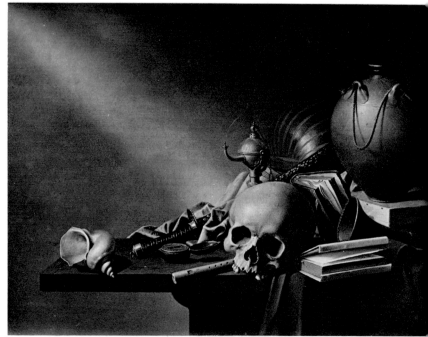

1256 STEENWYCK, HERMAN   STILL LIFE

146 STORCK   VIEW ON THE MAES

89 SUSTERMAN
PORTRAIT OF FERDINAND II OF TUSCANY AND HIS WIFE

3227 SUSTERMAN
PORTRAIT OF A FLORENTINE NOBLE

1699 SWEERTZ   A FAMILY GROUP

949 TENIERS, DAVID I   ROCKY LANDSCAPE

TENIERS, DAVID II   A MUSIC PARTY

TENIERS, DAVID II   MONEY CHANGERS

158   TENIERS, DAVID II   THE COMPANIONS

242 TENIERS, DAVID II   PLAYERS AT TRIC-TRAC, OR BACKGAMMOR

TENIERS, DAVID II   AN OLD WOMAN PEELING A PEAR

TENIERS, DAVID II   TENIERS' CHÂTEAU AT PERCK

857 TENIERS, DAVID II   SPRING

858 TENIERS, DAVID II   SUMME

859 TENIERS, DAVID II   AUTUMN

860 TENIERS, DAVID II   WINT

1 TENIERS, DAVID II   RIVER SCENE

2 TENIERS, DAVID II   THE SURPRISE (LA SURPRISE FÂCHEUSE)

863 TENIERS, DAVID II   DIVES IN HELL (LE MAUVAIS RICHE)

950 TENIERS, DAVID II   THE CONVERSATION

51 TENIERS, DAVID II   PLAYING AT BOWLS

52 TENIERS, DAVID II   THE VILLAGE FÊTE

953   TENIERS, DAVID II   THE TOPER

2599   TENIERS, DAVID II   A VISIT TO THE DOCTOR

500 TENIERS, DAVID II SCHOOL OF   THE CARD PLAYERS

2601   TENIERS, DAVID II SCHOOL OF
AN OLD WOMAN READING

864   TER BORCH   THE GUITAR LESSON

1399   TER BORCH   PORTRAIT OF A GENTLEMAN

896 TER BORCH. THE PEACE OF MÜNSTER

4596 TER BORCH
PORTRAIT (HERMANNA VAN DER CRUYSSE?)

4164 TER BRUYGHEN   JACOB AND LABAN

3964 TOCQUÉ
PORTRAIT OF A YOUNG FRENCH
GENTLEMAN

4097 TOCQUÉ
PORTRAIT OF A MAN IN A FLOWERED VEST

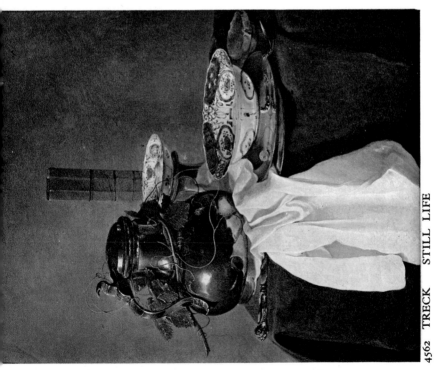

4562 TRECK STILL LIFE

2081   UNKNOWN ARTIST
LULLI AND THE MUSICIANS OF THE
FRENCH COURT (?)

1017 UNKNOWN, D.D.V.   A LANDSCAPE

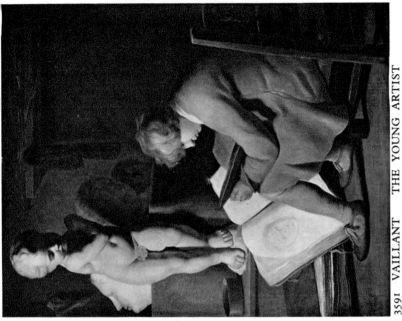

3591 VAILLANT   THE YOUNG ARTIST

1291 VALDÉS LEAL   THE ASSUMPTION OF THE VIRGIN

197　VELAZQUEZ　PORTRAIT OF PHILIP IV HUNTING THE WILD BOAR

45 VELAZQUEZ PORTRAIT OF PHILIP IV WHEN ELDERLY

1129 VELAZQUEZ   PORTRAIT OF PHILIP IV WHEN YOUNG

1148 VELAZQUEZ CHRIST AT THE COLUMN

1315 VELAZQUEZ
PORTRAIT OF ADMIRAL
PULIDO-PAREJA

1375 VELAZQUEZ   THE HOUSE OF MARTHA

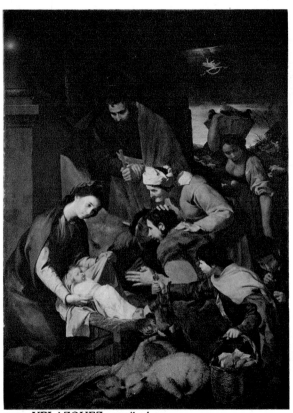

232 VELAZQUEZ, ascribed to
THE ADORATION OF THE SHEPHERDS

2057   VELAZQUEZ   VENUS AND CUPID : " THE ROKEBY VENUS "

867　VELDE, A. VAN DE　　THE FARM COTTAGE

868　VELDE, A. VAN DE　　THE FORD

869 VELDE, A. VAN DE   FROST SCENE

82 VELDE, A. VAN DE   FOREST SCENE

983   VELDE, A. VAN DE   BAY HORSE

984   VELDE, A. VAN DE   LANDSCAPE WITH CATTLE

1348 VELDE, A. VAN DE
LANDSCAPE WITH A GOAT AND KID

2572 VELDE, A. VAN DE   THE LITTLE FARM

1255 VELDE, J. VAN DE   STILL LIFE

149 VELDE, W. VAN DE   A CALM AT SEA

150 VELDE, W. VAN DE   GALE AT SEA

870 VELDE, W. VAN DE   SHIPPING IN A CALM

871 VELDE, W. VAN DE   COAST SCENE : CALM

872 VELDE, W. VAN DE   SHIPPING OFF THE COAST

873 VELDE, W. VAN DE   COAST OF SCHEVENINGEN

874 VELDE, W. VAN DE   CALM AT SEA

875 VELDE, W. VAN DE   A LIGHT BREEZE

876 VELDE, W. VAN DE   A GALE

VELDE, W. VAN DE   SHIPS AT ANCHOR

VELDE, W. VAN DE   RIVER SCENE

979 VELDE, W. VAN DE   SHIPPING

980 VELDE, W. VAN DE   A CALM : VESSELS SALUTING

81 VELDE, W. VAN DE   SHIPS IN A STORM

573 VELDE, W. VAN DE   SEASCAPE

2574 VELDE, W. VAN DE   CALM: SHIPPING

2575 VELSEN   A MUSICAL PARTY

1009 VERBEECK, Ascribed to   THE OLD GREY HUNTER

2568 VERMEER   LADY SEATED AT THE VIRGINALS

1383 VERMEER   LADY STANDING AT THE VIRGINALS

850 VERMEULEN   A SCENE ON THE ICE

1 VERNET   A SEAPORT

236 VERNET CASTLE OF SANT' ANGELO, ROME

1057 VERNET LANDSCAPE

393 VERNET MEDITERRANEAN SEAPORT

3134 VERSCHURING BATTLE PIECE

1312 VICTOORS   THE VILLAGE COBBLER

3025 VLIEGER   MOUTH OF A RIVER

4455 VLIEGER VESSELS IN AN ESTUARY

1168 VLIET
PORTRAIT OF A PROFESSOR (?)

3475 VROOM   LANDSCAPE

1002 WALSCAPPELLE
      FLOWERS, INSECTS AND STRAWBERRIES

2897 WATTEAU LA GAMME D'AMOUR

2962 WATTEAU—STUDIO OF
L'ACCORD PARFAIT

4079 WATTEAU—SCHOOL OF   FÊTE CHAMPÊTRE

1096 WEENIX, JAN BAPTIST   HUNTING SCENE

238 WEENIX, JAN THE YOUNGER
DEAD GAME AND A DOG

70 WEIER BATTLE SCENE

3909 WERFF   THE REPOSE IN EGYPT

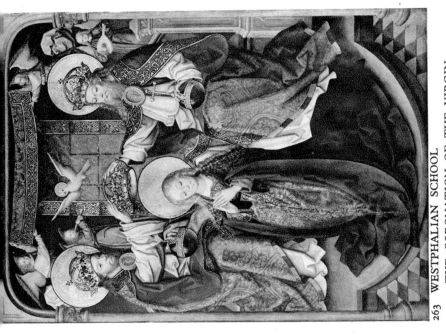

263 WESTPHALIAN SCHOOL
THE CORONATION OF THE VIRGIN

2151 WESTPHALIAN SCHOOL

2154 WESTPHALIAN SCHOOL

1342 WET LANDSCAPE

654 WEYDEN THE MAGDALEN

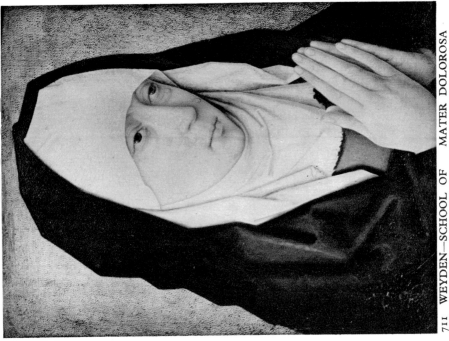

711 WEYDEN—SCHOOL OF MATER DOLOROSA

712 WEYDEN—SCHOOL OF ECCE HOMO

687　MASTER WILHELM, ascribed to
S. VERONICA

1007　WILS　　ROCKY LANDSCAPE

1053 WITTE   INTERIOR OF A CHURCH, PROBABLY AT DELFT

3682 WITTE—After   THE FISH MARKET

1871 WOUTERS   NYMPS AND SATYRS

1345 WOUWERMAN, J.   LANDSCAPE

878 WOUWERMAN, P.   HALT OF THE OFFICERS

879 WOUWERMAN, P.   INTERIOR OF A STABLE

880 WOUWERMAN, P.   ON THE SEA SHORE

881 WOUWERMAN, P.
GATHERING FAGGOTS

WOUWERMAN, P.   LANDSCAPE WITH BEGGARS

3 WOUWERMAN, P.   SANDBANK ON A RIVER

975 WOUWERMAN, P.   THE STAG HUNT

976 WOUWERMAN, P.   A BATTLE, CAVALRY AND INFANTRY

1060 WOUWERMAN, P. TWO VEDETTES ON THE WATCH

2282 WOUWERMAN, P. BOHEMIANS

2554 WOUWERMAN, P.   SHOEING A HORSE IN THE OPEN

883 WYNANTS   LANDSCAPE WITH FIGURES AND ANIMALS

884 WYNANTS LANDSCAPE WITH FIGURES

971 WYNANTS HILLY COUNTRY

972 WYNANTS   LANDSCAPE WITH DEAD TREES

2532 WYNANTS   A WOMAN DRIVING SHEEP THROUGH AN ARCHWAY

2533 WYNANTS   A SANDY LANE

1864 YSENBRANDT   THE VIRGIN AND CHILD

2585 YSENBRANDT   S. MARY MAGDALENE

230 ZURBARAN   A FRANCISCAN

1930 ZURBARAN   PORTRAIT OF A LADY AS S. MARGARET